How to Write a Résumé:
Finding a Job in Any Job Market

ALSO BY SARA SALAM

The Mind Is Just Like A Muscle: A Self-Help Book For Teens On Growing Up in Modern America

My Truth Journal

If Water Were Fire, A Novel

If Love Were Salt, A Novel

Love Isn't Linear: A Collection of Poems About Modern Love

My Newport: A Collection of Poems About Newport Beach, California

Remember When: A Collection of Poems By A Lovestruck Teen Who Had The Courage to Dream

How to Write a Résumé:

Finding a Job in Any Job Market

By Sara Salam

The Peacock Pen Press

2021

Copyright © 2021 Sara Salam

All rights reserved. No part of this book may be used in any manner whatsoever without written permission, except in the case of brief quotations and reviews.

ISBN: 978-1-953636-06-5 (Paperback)
ISBN: 978-1-953636-07-2 (Hardcover)
ISBN: 978-1-953636-08-9 (eBook)

Library of Congress Control Number: 2021904320
1. Job Hunting & Careers
2. Business & Money
3. Job Markets & Advice
4. Résumés
5. Self-Help
6. Personal Success

Book cover design by Booklerk.
Author portrait by Christina Wehbe.
Edited by Anna Alger.

Icons from the Noun Project: Exercise by Miho Suzuki-Robinson; Hammer and nails by Made; Resume by Branken; Book by Toli; Crystal Ball by Made; Drone by Ranah Pixel Studio; Book by Cantasia; landscape by ProSymbols; bonus by DinosoftLab; jobs search by Andri Graphic; chart by Norbert Kucsera; coin by icon 54; professional by Flatart; Exercise by IconMark; graduation by Vectors Market; explosion by Nick Abrams; Camera by Tinashe Mugayi; bow and arrow by Line Icons Pro.

Printed by The Peacock Pen Press in the United States of America.
First Printing Edition 2021.

© 2021 Sara Salam

www.bysarasalam.com/careerconsulting

@bysarasalam

Sara Salam

For all the job seekers making it happen.

CONTENTS

Introduction — 1

Part I: The Job Hunting Landscape — 7

Part II: Your Career Chronicle — 27

Part III: Planning for the (Near and Distant) Future — 53

Conclusion — 70

Bonus Content — 72

Thank You! — 78

Acknowledgments — 79

About the Author — 80

References — 81

INTRODUCTION

IT'S HARD ALL AROUND

The job market is a chaotic place for job seekers and employers alike. Having been on both sides, I empathize with the challenges both groups face in the hiring process.

Hiring is hard. By most statistical (and anecdotal) accounts, making a hiring decision is a 50-50 situation for employers. As a job seeker, this can be heartbreaking to hear. Even if you do get hired, there's a good chance it won't work out. I don't say this to be negative, but to illustrate the reality of the hiring landscape. Rather than focus on what could be construed as negative, this book explores the opportunities for job seekers.

My goal is not to help you find your dream job. My goal is to help you understand the forces that influence hiring processes in modern times, and how you can best present yourself as a working professional to hiring managers and recruiters.

> My goal is not to help you find your dream job. My goal is to help you understand the forces that influence hiring processes in modern times, and how you can best present yourself as a working professional to hiring managers and recruiters.

A QUICK NOTE ABOUT ME

I have hired 3,000+ people in various positions over the last decade. As a former recruiter and human resources professional of ten years, I know what employers look for when reviewing résumés, cover letters, and any of the content that helps hiring managers and recruiters make hiring decisions. In addition to my author business (fiction, nonfiction, and poetry), I consult with job seekers and employers on hiring practices and principles.

I worked in professional sports for seven seasons—five with the Boston Red Sox and two with the LA Clippers—where my responsibilities focused on recruiting, diversity and inclusion initiatives, training and development, program management, and other generalist duties. I also dabbled in psychometrics (think Myers-Briggs, Enneagram, and alternatives) and the start-up world. My purpose is to educate, entertain and empower through the power of story, which includes helping you write and revise your professional narrative. Telling stories is a distinctly human trait (as far as scientific studies have revealed), and in these pages you'll learn tools and techniques for telling your own story as a working professional.

WHO THIS BOOK IS FOR

I wrote this book for any job seeker looking for inspiration on how to refresh their approach to the job search process. While the contents of this book focus on what I call career chronicling (including résumés, cover letters, and LinkedIn profiles), it also shows job seekers a different way to approach the job hunting process and how to present themselves to employers. This book is for job seekers who are stuck on deciding what to include on a résumé (what you EXCLUDE that is more important than what you INCLUDE). It's for job seekers who haven't been in the job market for a while and need an update on what's what. It's for new grads, returning servicepeople, the formerly incarcerated, and parents who took a hiatus before returning to the workforce.

Most people will engage in a job search process at some point in their lifetime. There is no one way to find a job. There is no one way to write a résumé. There is no one way to interview. In this book, I highlight the strategy I have found most effective in my nearly ten years of experience as a recruiter, human resources professional, and consultant. I don't expose any big secrets; instead, I offer a point of view that focuses on job seekers' individual strengths and experiences, while educating them on the markets they are working in. I encourage job seekers to focus on what they can control. Put simply, it's their professional narrative.

WHAT THIS BOOK IS NOT

This book is not a recipe for writing a résumé. Everyone has a different recipe. Rather, this book provides guidance on what to consider when you're writing your own recipe, how to determine what ingredients to use, and advises what proportions are likely to taste better. This is a book of strategy, not transactional instruction.

This book is not about how to "cheat the system." It's not about beating algorithms or sneaking to the front of the lunch line that is the candidate queue. It is about positioning yourself in the most effective way possible so that hiring managers and recruiters know right away that they should consider you for the opportunity in question.

This is not a book about "faking it until you make it." This is not a book about interviewing, negotiating job offers, or networking. All of these topics are important, and I encourage you to research them to supplement your knowledge.

If you're looking for specific services related to (re)starting your job search and other related support, you can find my information at bysarasalam.com/careerconsulting for a consultation.

HOW THIS BOOK IS STRUCTURED

In Part I, we explore the various nuances of the job hunting landscape, which includes understanding the job market in both good times and bad. Depending on when you first read this book, your job market outlook could be totally different from when you read it again a few years later. The goal is to learn about market forces and how they control (or don't control) your job opportunities.

In Part II, the most workshop-y section of the book, you'll learn about career chronicles , what it means, and how to use it when developing your professional narrative. We'll reference specific tips and tricks for curating your content (résumés, cover letters, LinkedIn profiles, etc.) so you can create a cohesive, consistent career chronicle in the marketplace as you conduct your job search.

In Part III, we'll consider what the future could look like given the recent developments in job hunting and in corporate America as a whole. While we can't predict it, the future of job hunting will likely be dictated by a combination of market forces, technology, and the pace of adaptation of technology by employers and job seekers alike.

But first, let's start by taking a look at the job hunting landscape, in good times and bad.

PART I: THE JOB HUNTING LANDSCAPE

DEFINITIONS

The Job Market

The job market, also known as the labor market, is the market in which employers search for employees and employees search for jobs. The job market isn't a physical place like a grocery store or bazaar; it's a concept that represents the competition and dynamics between different labor forces.

The job market can expand or contract depending on the demand for labor and the available supply of workers within the overall economy. More factors impacting the job market include the needs of a specific industry, the need for a particular education level or skill set, and required job functions. The job market is an important component of any economy and is directly tied to the demand for goods and services.

Unemployment

The job market is also directly related to the unemployment rate. The unemployment rate is the percentage of people in the labor force who are not currently employed, but who are actively seeking a job.

Unemployment is often used as a measure of the health of the economy. The most frequent measure of unemployment is the unemployment rate, also known as the U-3 rate, which is the number of unemployed people divided by the number of people in the labor force.

Another lesser-known metric for unemployment is the U-6, which includes groups such as discouraged workers, or those who have stopped looking for a new job, and the underemployed, or people who are working part time because they can't find full-time work.

In fact, there are SIX different ways the Bureau of Labor Statistics measures unemployment. (The BLS calls all but U-3 metrics of "labor underutilization." U-6 can be referred to as the "real" unemployment rate because it includes discouraged workers, or people who left the workforce because they couldn't find a job.) We won't get into all six here, but it's worth noting to illustrate that unemployment isn't as straightforward as joblessness, but in fact has far more implications than we might be aware of.

Low unemployment rate

- Low unemployment is usually regarded as a positive sign for the economy.
- A very low rate of unemployment, however, can have negative consequences, such as inflation and reduced productivity.
- When the labor market reaches a point where each additional job doesn't create enough productivity to cover its cost, then an output gap, or slack, happens.

High unemployment rate

- High unemployment indicates the economy is operating below full capacity and is inefficient; this will lead to lower output and incomes. This is typically a negative sign for the economy as a whole.
- The unemployed are also unable to purchase as many goods, and thus will contribute to lower spending and lower output. A rise in unemployment can cause a negative multiplier effect.
- The higher the unemployment rate, the greater the supply of labor in the overall job market.

"Healthy" unemployment rate

The level at which unemployment equals positive output is highly debated. However, economists suggest that when the U.S. unemployment rate drops below 5%, the economy is very close to or at full capacity. At 3.5%, one could argue the level of unemployment is too low, and the U.S. economy is becoming inefficient.

WHAT DOES A GOOD JOB MARKET LOOK LIKE? WHAT DOES A BAD JOB MARKET LOOK LIKE?

As we've seen, there are general economic terms and metrics to describe positive and negative market conditions for both employers and employees. As we've also seen, there is a lot of gray area and nuance, depending on which metrics you look at and how you apply them.

The short answer to these questions is, it depends. Mostly, it depends on you, a member of the workforce, and your goals. Let's assume your goal is to find a job. How you look for a job in a good job market will likely be different than how you look for a job in a bad job market.

To some degree the terms "good job market" and "bad job market" are misnomers, because what might be a good job market for you could be a bad job market for your coworker. How? Labor forces, including supply and demand, affect skill sets differently. For example, your friend Ash might be a software engineer; depending on supply and demand, he may or may not have more job options given his skill set. The same is true for your sister Jessica, who is a nurse. But also consider Tavio, who is a hospitality professional. Nursing credentials and hospitality credentials are viewed  and applied differently, which shows why, even if both individuals are applying for jobs in a "good job market," one might find a job faster in their given industry than the other.

Now that we're sufficiently familiar with these terms, let's turn back to our economic definitions as a baseline so we're speaking consistently about how labor forces interact with each other.

Aside: I'd like to foreshadow a point here about transferable skills. While nursing and hospitality roles vary quite differently in terms of their vocabulary (medical versus entertainment), systems (charting versus point of service), and the environment where work is performed (hospital versus hotel or restaurant), there are similarities, too. Namely, the skill of customer service: ensuring the client or patient's needs and expectations are met.

LOOKING FOR A JOB IN A GOOD JOB MARKET

This might surprise you. It's still hard! Even in the best of times, both employers and job seekers still face challenges.

Let's go back to around 2017-2018. It was a time when unemployment was the lowest it had been in years—about 4%. It would get as low as 3.5% in early 2020, before the coronavirus pandemic. The job market was booming. That should have been a good thing!

While it was statistically great for the economy, employers argued otherwise.

Their reality: although there were lots of jobs to be filled, they claimed there were not enough qualified people to fill them. 65% of recruiters reported a talent shortage, saying they couldn't find the right people to fill their open positions.

The consequences?

Employers consistently made bad hires. 95% of companies admitted to hiring the wrong people each year. As a result, turnover rates and expensive costs associated with productivity increased.

To put a dollar value to it, that's between $483 billion and $605 billion in lost productivity and 23% in lost revenue in 2017 alone. In general, to replace a single bad hire costs at least 30% of their salary, all-inclusive.

Considered together, we can see that beyond finding a job, what's important is finding a job that mutually benefits both the employer and employee. With humans doing the hiring, it's a crapshoot. There's a lot of reasons why this is true, which are beyond the scope of this book.

For our purposes, the takeaway is that even in a good job market, in modern times it's difficult to get hired by a company AND stay for the long term. ("Long term" is loosely defined here, but let's call it over five years of service.)

In fact, job hopping is relatively "normal." In three surveys by Jobvite (2014-2016 survey years), between 34% to 35% of all job seekers reported that they change jobs after one to five years. As the economy ebbs and flows, so does perspective on how hard the prior year has been for job seekers.

These facts and figures are not meant to discourage you. The intent is to show you that "good" and "bad" are relative when talking about the job market. You can't control the forces of the labor market—it's simply impossible. But you can control how you engage with it and how you present yourself to potential employers.

Before we get into how you can do that, let's look at what a bad job market could look like.

LOOKING FOR A JOB IN A BAD JOB MARKET

In both good times and bad, there are always going to be winners and losers. Even when unemployment rates are at record lows, there are still people who are unemployed. Let's assume the "worst-case scenario bad job market" is a recession. Even if you haven't yet faced the effects of a recession during your career, it's good to be prepared. In my lifetime alone, I've witnessed three recessions, including two as an adult: in 2008 and in 2020. I graduated college in 2010, and my job prospects as a new grad were certainly affected.

> You can't control the forces of the labor market–it's simply impossible. But you can control how you engage with it and how you present yourself to potential employers.

What does a recession look like?

During a typical recession (if we can call it that), regardless of the cause, as the recession spreads, more and more businesses curtail their activities or fail altogether, and as a result, lay off their workers. This makes sense, given that payroll accounts for as much as 30% of any business' expenses.

In a recession, because many businesses across many different industries and markets are failing all at once, the number of unemployed workers looking for new jobs increases rapidly. The supply of labor available for immediate hire goes up, but the demand from businesses to hire new workers goes down. In a perfect, frictionless, functioning market, economists would expect such an increase in supply and decrease in demand to result in lower prices (in this case, the average wage) but not necessarily a lower total number of jobs once the price adjusts.

However, this doesn't necessarily happen during recessions. The unemployed workers face difficulty in finding new jobs, and the result is a surplus of labor of many kinds that can last for several months.

Keep in mind

It's important to note that the figures produced and shared by economists and statisticians ignore differences in labor and capital. The intention of these folks is to produce aggregate macroeconomic data, including unemployment rates. The reality is, not all jobs, companies, and markets are affected equally during good and bad times.

In classical or "ideal" business cycles (i.e., textbook theory and not necessarily real life), the number of openings decreases and the number of applicants increases, or vice versa. During the coronavirus pandemic, however, the impact of crisis disproportionately affected employers and job seekers alike. Some industries and firms were devastated, while others thrived, were unaffected, or rebounded. The job market witnessed a high rate of jobs disappearing and reappearing at the same time, mixed with an unusual economic downturn.

Not all recessions are created equal

Some industries and businesses (and their workforces) are hit harder than others in any given recession. For example, during the Great Recession that began circa 2008, construction, manufacturing, and the finance, insurance, and real estate sectors saw the greatest increases in unemployment. In contrast, the largest jump in unemployment in 2020 was felt in the leisure and hospitality industry, as the economy felt the impacts of the COVID-19 pandemic. These workers faced the challenge of finding jobs in other businesses—or even other industries—that suit their abilities and experience.

When unemployment peaked in April 2020, 78% of unemployed workers reported they were on temporary layoffs, the highest level ever reported. For context, temporary layoffs are normally 10-15% of unemployment.

But in this recession, the huge rise in temporary layoffs created lots of uncertainty about whether and how soon people would be able to go back to work.

By October 2020, the temporary unemployment number dropped back to 29%. These wild swings skewed some essential measures of the labor market, like the unemployment rate.

How do we move forward?

Clearing the surplus of unemployed workers in the markets of each of the many types of labor requires getting the right workers matched up to the right jobs, rather than simply balancing generic aggregate workers with generic aggregate jobs from a macro perspective. Workers (and capital goods) across different jobs and industries are not interchangeable blocks that can simply be plugged into the first available opening. The puzzle pieces need to fit together properly, or the machine of the economy simply won't go back together.

This process of sorting the right workers into the right jobs takes time, and requires simultaneously sorting the right tools, equipment, buildings, and other capital needed to complement those workers' skills and abilities into the hands of businesses that can use all these resources together in legitimately productive (and profitable) activities.

Moreover, both of these sorting processes require flexibility on the part of workers and employers. They must be flexible not just in terms of the prices, wages, and quantities supplied and demanded, around which classroom economic models revolve, but also in terms of the ability to move and combine different types of workers and capital goods between firms and markets. If the markets for labor and capital goods are sufficiently flexible in these ways, then the pain of the recession might be short lived after the initial shock.

> If the markets for labor and capital goods are sufficiently flexible in these ways, then the pain of the recession might be short lived after the initial shock.

An interesting digression: Corporations

In his book, *Sapiens: A Brief History of Humankind*, Yuval Noah Harari makes a compelling observation about corporations and the role they play in our economics:

"Ever since the Cognitive Revolution, Sapiens have been living in a dual reality. On the one hand, the objective reality of rivers, trees, and lions; on the other hand, the imagined reality of gods, nations, and corporations. As time went by, the imagined reality became ever more powerful, so that today the survival of rivers, trees and lions depends on the grace of imagined entities such as the United States and Google."

For one thing, corporations are a figment of our collective imaginations—a legal fiction, as termed by lawyers.

Before the creation of corporations, people themselves were personally held liable for loans, private property, and transactions gone wrong; a scenario which, as you can imagine, discouraged entrepreneurship. People were afraid to start businesses and absorb economic risks, and rightly so.

Today, as has been the trend over the past few centuries, such companies have become dominant players on the economic scene. It's easy to forget these entities only exist in our imaginations. And as illustrated by many corporations' behaviors, they often do.

How did companies become such a driving force in our world's economy? By telling effective stories, and convincing people to believe in them. It's through this belief that millions of strangers are able to cooperate and work towards common goals. These ideas are concretized by company vision, mission, and values.

What's ironic is, (most) companies operate with the bottom line in mind, not the interest of its people. When in fact, the company is composed of—you guessed it—people. The primary customers are, in general, people. I call this the people's paradox.

Many of us operate with the assumption that companies have the best interest of their employees in mind. Given the company itself functions in the interest of profit, we need to be mindful of these implications and how they affect us as people, not as assets or capital.

ANOTHER WAY TO LOOK AT IT

What's interesting about this is, the same idea is applicable to the job market even when we're *not* in an economic recession.

Consider the following:

For the past few decades, companies focused on hiring for competencies, or the past demonstration of skills presumed to indicate successful performance in a specific job. We could say the workplace during this time was relatively stable and jobs were relatively consistent.

Today, the business world looks different and is certainly more convoluted. We'll get into exactly how in Part III. For now, it's important to note hiring decisions have always been difficult to make, in good times and bad. So, then, how do we improve?

I'd argue **transferable skills** are critical for employees and employers to understand when it comes to job fit and "hireability." We'll discuss the idea of transferable skills and focus on what it means for job hunting in Part II.

Why this will be hard to do

Humans are risk-averse creatures. We are social. We are anxious. We often act out of fear.

Often, we forget that those running our businesses are human beings. First and foremost, before we are employees, before we are business owners, we are human beings. We all have physical needs, mental needs, emotional needs, etc., that don't disappear once work begins.

Corporations as we know them arose in Britain with the Joint Stock Companies Act of 1844. The power to control them thus passed from the government to the courts. In 1855, shareholders were awarded limited liability: their personal assets were protected from the consequences of their corporate actions. In 1886, a landmark decision by a US court recognized the corporation as a 'natural person' under law.

Two-thirds of Americans have favorable opinions of major companies and even more hold positive views of small businesses, according to the Public Affairs Council's 2015 Public Affairs Pulse Survey. The organization reports that "while people think big businesses provide useful products and services and serve customers well, they are critical of companies for paying high executive salaries and not doing enough to protect the environment, create jobs and support communities."

As humans navigating this landscape, it's critical we recognize what fundamentally makes us human, what unique characteristics define the human condition, and what the implications are for us at work, and quite frankly, at home as well.

These sorting processes involving jobs and workers will require time and market flexibility. The common denominator: patience.

In Part II, we will focus on what we can control, which is how we present ourselves to employers and the story or stories we tell about our professional selves and our workplace potential.

In Part III, we will explore and ask questions about what future job markets could look like and how we as job seekers can best participate and prepare.

But first, let's take a look at the unique challenges employers and job seekers face in modern markets and workplaces.

CHALLENGES FOR EMPLOYERS

Today, the process of applying for a job is almost too easy. Point, click, submit. This results in a high volume of applicants that dilutes quality, requiring more time and effort for employers to find the needle in the haystack, and therefore reducing the likelihood that the applications of those actually best suited for a role will even be seen by a hiring manager. Only 2% of applicants will be called for an interview for the average job opening. 48% of businesses say their quality hires come from employee referrals. As a result, most companies are only considering talent that has an existing relationship with a current employee.

What's more, employers are having difficulty drawing correlation between the résumé content of their candidates and jobs that aren't an exact "plug-and-play" match.

A study by Leadership IQ revealed that only 11% of people are terminated because of poor technical skills, which is the basis of what we learn from résumés. What's more, this content is self-reported, and therefore also inherently biased. As  employers, we see what job seekers want us to see. Finally, there is a lack of depth to résumés and job descriptions, neither of which tells the whole story of what's required of the job or the person doing the job, respectively.

The speed at which jobs are being created is accelerating at such a rapid pace—39,300 jobs were created in California in April 2018 alone—while the similarly rapid pace of technology development is constantly changing the requisite skills employees need to perform these newly created positions. (Even during recessions in both 2001 and 2008, the number of job openings quickly dropped below 4 million and continued to sink for months. In June 2020, in contrast, we observed an increase to 5.9 million job openings, climbing to 6.6 million openings in July. This is double the 2009 average and more job openings than in any year from the time the data was first collected in 2000 until 2017, though fewer openings than in the prior two years.)

Consider the manufacturing sector, where jobs that were once physical labor intensive not ten years ago have now shifted to "bot operators"—a completely different job model. Employers are thus challenged with identifying prospective employees that are the "right fit" yet who may not have mirror-image past experience to refer to as a baseline. The key? Transferable skills.

	February 2018	February 2019	February 2020	March 2020	April 2020	May 2020	June 2020	November 2020
Unemployment Rate	4.10%	3.80%	3.50%	4.40%	14.70%	13.30%	11.10%	6.70%
Job Openings	6.1M	7.1M	6.9M	6.2M	5M	5.4M	5.9M	6.7M
Job Openings Rate	3.90%	4.50%	4.30%	3.90%	3.70%	3.90%	4.10%	4.50%
Hires	5.5M	5.7M	5.9M	5.2M	3.5M	6.5M	6.7M	5.8M
Separations	5.2M	5.6M	5.6M	14.5M	9.9M	4.1M	4.8M	5.1M
Quits Rate	2.20%	2.30%	2.30%	1.80%	1.40%	1.60%	1.90%	2.20%
Layoffs/Discharges Rate	1.10%	1.20%	1.20%	7.50%	5.90%	1.40%	1.40%	1.20%

*Largest monthly decrease in separations took place in May 2020
*Largest monthly increase in hires took place in May 2020
*Lowest number of hires recorded took place in April 2020

Source: BLS.gov

ASIDE: BUREAU OF LABOR STATISTICS DATA

As you can see in the table above, even during the recession brought about by the coronavirus pandemic, the number of job openings and job openings rates remained consistently high. In April 2020, job openings totaled 5 million with a job openings rate of 3.7%, the lowest during the calendar year; these numbers are still really high. In fact, they are comparable to those in June 2015, when the job openings totaled 5.2 million and the job openings rate was 3.6%.

The takeaway: even when unemployment rates are high, the number of job openings can still be high as well. In these instances, employers and job seekers alike must consider talent as capital with transferable skills and understand what that means for productivity and workplace potential.

CHALLENGES FOR JOB SEEKERS

Studies show recruiters today only take six seconds to review a résumé. Today, the résumé is simply a formality to send to HR to make sure the applicant is a "real person". Furthermore, a candidate could give the best thirty-minute interview, a very short period of time where they are on their best behavior, whether it's their true self or not. How can we base hiring decisions on these fleeting factors, given the cost of replacing a poor-performing employee is expensive at best, and bankruptcy-inducing at worst?

We need to be intentional about matching the best person to the job by also bearing in mind how their natural behaviors align with the behaviors of the job. Skills and knowledge evolve over time, and can be taught (you can use Google to learn almost anything these days), but you can't teach someone to be a different person or how their human self shows up in the workplace. We should embrace an approach that considers the whole self, not just what we see at first glance on a résumé. Remember: talent is largely personality in the right place, and most talent management problems are solved once you get the right person in the right job.

A 2017 Gallup study found that roughly 30% of American employees felt occupied or enthused by their jobs, while the other 70% weren't utilizing their full potential.

There's that word again: *potential*. How can we measure potential reliably? Through transferable skills.

In Part II, we will unpack this term "transferable skills" in the context of your career chronicle and how you present yourself to potential employers.

TAKEAWAYS

- Just because the job market is good by economic standards—i.e., unemployment is low—doesn't mean the right people are being hired for the right job
    - Low unemployment does not equal low turnover.
- For the job seeker, this means that it's most important for you to understand your value, identify what kind of work makes you happy and productive, and go find that job or those jobs.
- In good times AND bad times, there will always be winners and losers.
- Transferable skills are key to understanding how you as a job seeker add value to a prospective employer.

PART II: YOUR CAREER CHRONICLE

After we define career chronicling, we'll get into how to identify the core of your professional narrative—your "why." We'll then spend some time taking a deep dive into résumé content and a different approach to thinking about what to include and exclude. Finally, we'll touch on cover letters and LinkedIn profiles, and how they connect to your career narrative.

WHAT IS CAREER CHRONICLING?

Let's break down this term. We all know what a *career* is: an occupation undertaken for a significant period of a person's life with opportunities for progress. The term implies longevity, a tenured commitment to a chosen profession. In modern times, the trajectory of a career can pivot and change, especially given the rate at which technology changes or is created, and how that affects which jobs exist altogether or how work itself is performed. (We'll talk more about this in Part III.) For now, let's think about a career as a commitment to work.

Chronicling, simply, is the reporting or recounting of a story. Think *The Chronicles of Narnia* by C.S. Lewis. "Chronicle" is another word for story.

So, taken together, a career chronicle is the narrative you present to potential employers in the context of professional skills and experience.

How do you build a professional narrative? What story are you sharing with employers? The short answer: it depends. The long answer: it depends on the job you are applying for.

YOUR PROFESSIONAL NARRATIVE

Your professional narrative is your professional story. It captures not only your work history, but most importantly, WHY and HOW your career path looks the way it does. Your professional narrative can be told in many mediums. The most obvious and legacied form is your résumé.

With the modern advent of new/digital/social media, there are more opportunities than ever to share your professional narrative. These include your LinkedIn profile, your personal/professional website, your YouTube channel, your Pinterest boards, etc.

In this book, we'll focus specifically on how to build your résumé, since this content is the most universally applicable for the typical job seeker.

But first, let's discuss how to write your professional narrative. Your output will be useful in building not only your résumé, but other career chronicling materials as well, including your LinkedIn profile, professional bio, and the like.

Your Professional "Why"

What is this?

Your professional narrative begins with your "why": your purpose for your chosen profession. While it's not something you will necessarily reference verbatim on your career chronicle materials, developing your why is a helpful exercise in framing your story and your mindset as you apply for jobs.

Leadership and thought leader Simon Sinek explains why some companies, movements, and individuals inspire, while others do not. We'll build off this notion of inspiration to think through your professional "why."

Using the concept of the Golden Circle, Sinek highlights the differences between what we do, how we do it, and...dun dun dun...why we do it. What is our purpose, our cause, our belief? The biology of the human brain explains our process of thought as consumers, how the limbic brain and the neocortex work together to express how we feel 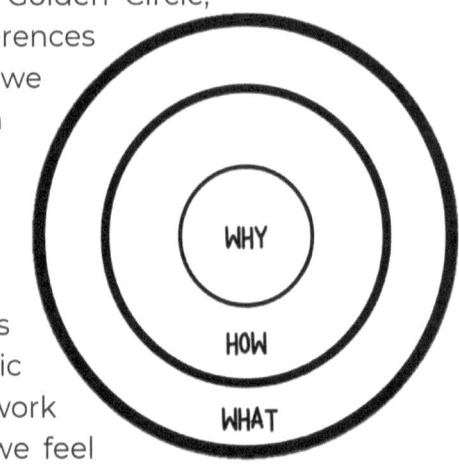 about any given product or service and how that drives our behavior.

For example, consider how Apple positions their products versus other computer companies, who are perfectly qualified to produce similar products but don't have close to the market share Apple does. What's the difference? It's their why.

The average computer company: "We make great computers. We design everything so that it's easy to use and user friendly. Want to buy one?"

Apple: "Everything we do, we believe in challenging the status quo, we believe in thinking differently. We design everything so that it's easy to use and user friendly. We just happen to make good computers. Want to buy one?"

Or, why did Martin Luther King lead the civil rights movement, when there were other perfectly qualified individuals at the time who could do so? It's the why.

Key takeaways:

- People don't buy what you do, they buy why you do it.
- The goal is not to do business with EVERYONE, but to do business with people who BELIEVE WHAT YOU BELIEVE.

The same ideas apply to your job search.

- Employers don't hire you for what you do—they hire you for why you do it.
- The goal is not to apply for every job, but to find a job with a company that believes what you believe.

As Mark Twain once said, "The two most important days in your life are the day you are born, and the day you find out why."

What's your why?

Exercise: Figuring out your "why"

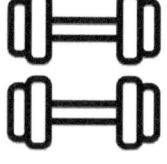

Read the following questions and free write your responses. Free writing means putting pen to paper (or fingers to keyboard) and writing consistently for at least three minutes, or until you've answered the question as thoroughly as possible.

There are no right or wrong answers. Write what comes to mind first and keep going. Don't overthink it.

1. What do you believe to be your greatest professional skills?
2. What do you believe to be your greatest contributions to your current and/or former employers?
3. What do you believe to be your purpose in life personally?
4. What do you believe to be your purpose in life professionally?
5. How do you connect with your customers/clients/coworkers? What strategies do you use to gain their trust?
6. How do you know your customers/clients/coworkers trust you?
7. Why are you in your chosen profession? What motivates you to do this type of work?

Review your responses. Is there a common theme? Are there words you repeat often?

Use these observations to formulate your why statement.

Try starting with *because*.

For example, my why statement is:

Because all human beings should feel safe and empowered in pursuit of their dreams.

You can omit *because* once you have determined what you want it to be. I find it helps with the brainstorming process. Keep in mind, it doesn't have to be set in stone initially. You will likely go through several iterations before you find one you commit to. It took me four versions before I landed on mine. Fear not!

Once you've identified your why, consider using it as a guideline for creating your career chronicle content. Remember, it won't necessarily be prominently displayed on your materials, but it will help share your career brand.

Let's start with how to build your résumé.

HOW TO BUILD A RÉSUMÉ

My general approach to building a résumé is to start wide and go narrow, meaning, identify the job you're applying for, then tailor your résumé accordingly.

Always, *always* tie all your content back to the main question you're answering for hiring managers and recruiters: why should they hire you for this job?

What is the purpose of a résumé?

The purpose of your résumé is threefold:

1. Tell your professional story.
2. Show your value.

3. Answer the question, why are you the best candidate for this position?

Tell your professional story

We are all storytellers. Today more than ever, we have the tools and resources to communicate to the world who we are, what we believe, what we like, what we don't like, and most relevant, our career aptitude and potential. In the professional world, LinkedIn has led the charge in recent years as a place to showcase experience, meet new professional contacts, and cultivate business relationships.

Your résumé should provide hiring managers and recruiters with your professional story.

Show your value

Your value includes your skills, experiences, certifications, education—anything that differentiates you or makes you attractive to an employer. These elements are the supporting details of your professional narrative. These include both quantitative and qualitative details, as both are important for adding supporting details to your narrative.

Answer the question, why are you the best candidate for this position?

When considering what to include or exclude from your résumé, always ask yourself this question.

In an ideal world, the résumé you submit for any given position should be the best representation of your professional narrative for that specific job. This necessitates matching up the requirements of the job description, both duties and responsibilities as well as skills and experience. I know this can be a tedious process, but once you iterate enough versions it will become a skill of your own.

Transferable Skills

Recall our discussion about transferable skills in Part I. Increasingly, transferable skills will be critical in telling your professional narrative. Why? Because skills—both hard and soft—are changing or evolving very quickly, and employers need to know how your skill set solves their current (and likely future) problems. This may seem like a tall order, and it is. In fact, and I don't mean for this to be discouraging, many employers don't know how to spot transferable skills on a résumé, as they are also caught in this web of incessant change and therefore also overwhelmed and paralyzed by Change (with a capital "C").

What do we do? We figure how the skill set we have transfers to our next job.

Consider the questions:

1. Where is the overlap?
2. What similarities exist between these jobs? What are the differences?
3. How would I describe these similarities?

Employees are like consumers

How do companies market to their consumers? Using today's sophisticated technologies, they use strategies like segmentation, targeting, positioning, and messaging.

What if we thought about employees as consumers? After all, employees invest more time and effort in their company and its brand than anyone else, and by extension are its most knowledgeable ambassadors.

As it turns out, some companies are doing just that. For example, given the gravitas of the virtual social community concept, one of the world's leading oil and gas companies uses a social customer service app to answer employee questions about using outside vendors.

By consulting the company's community, employees are able to get answers quickly from HR members, who can discuss policy, and from coworkers, who have previously sought outside vendors themselves. Because this particular customer service app plugs into the company's customer relationship management (CRM), employees can also pull down statistical data on topics such as the most popular vendors at any given point in time, and what they've been charging.

Professor Nick Kemsley, co-director of the Henley Business School Centre for HR Excellence, outlines five key ways employers can change their behaviors towards their employees and engage them in a consumer-minded way:

1. **Look outwards**. Change your HR approach to look outwards towards the employee, not inwards towards 'Core HR'. Ask yourself how many major initiatives in the last three years were really providing value to employees, versus value predominantly to your HR department (yes, that recent HRIS implementation, too).
2. **Get transformational, not transactional**. If your engagement practices are a set of activities or targets as a result of a survey, then they are reactive and transactional. To be transformational, there needs to be a deep belief in the power of people to contribute and that employees are integral to deliver business strategy.
3. **Your strategy must impact employees daily.** Consumers are fickle and expect great products and service, instantly. Your annual initiatives and programs won't work. Employees work in days and hours, not quarters or years.
4. **Engage managers**. Managers often get overlooked, but they're employees too. Too often, they're not ready for management and don't have the skill set or experience they need. Make managers part of the process of developing the strategy and enacting it with employees. Managers have more impact on changing the organization positively than leaders or executives.
5. **Get 'employee-specific'**. 'One size fits all' doesn't work for consumers, and it won't for employees either. Think about the times you've been mass-marketed to and you ignored it—your employees are no different. There needs to be a genuine interest in the individual employee.

Examples here might be helpful. For example, if I am a recruiter and I'm looking to make a career change into sales, how might I present myself in terms of transferable skills?

Every interview with a candidate is a sales call (whether the candidate knows it or not). Every time I screen a candidate, I'm not only qualifying their skill set, I'm also selling the company I represent as a potential employer. If that's not sales, I don't know what is.

Consider Simon Sinek's idea of the Golden Circle: people don't buy WHAT you do, they buy WHY you do it. Many companies make similar products or perform similar services, but they don't all do it for the same reasons. The same concept can be applied to employees: they don't work for you because of WHAT you do, but WHY you do it.

Give employees a reason to stay and treat them like your best customers. They'll keep coming back for more, just like your best customers would.

In my example of a recruiter applying for a sales position, how would I show this? Well, first I need to think about what information my future employer wants to know about my sales ability. In a word: numbers. This could be my number of hires, open reqs, closed reqs, turnover rates, salary ranges, retention, etc.

This idea might not be intuitive to everyone: frame your narrative in the mindset of the reader. Meaning, write your résumé as if it's summarizing everything the employer wants to know about their dream hire, and YOU are that dream hire. (Again, always, always be honest. This should go without saying.)

What a résumé is NOT

Your résumé is not a place to list every single thing you've ever done or achieved in your professional life. It's a curated representation of your work history that is specific to the job you're applying for. Your professional narrative should star you as the main character, with your bullet points describing key scenes, or milestones, in what has been your career story to date. What you choose to *exclude* is just as important as what you *include*. This isn't how we typically think about our literal life's work. Exclusion implies irrelevance. But this isn't necessarily a bad thing. Sometimes there are scenes in movies or books that are completely misplaced and don't contribute to the greater story arc. That's exactly what we're trying to avoid in constructing the plotline of your professional narrative.

> What you choose to *exclude* is just as important as what you *include*.

Formatting your résumé

Document Type

Text-based documents are most easily read by humans and applicant tracking systems, or ATSs. There's less opportunity for a faulty upload or download, and their content is searchable via word finders or keyword searches. As of this writing, most image-based files (.jpg, .png) are not searchable in most ATSs. The technology will likely evolve and change over time. For now, using file types like .doc, .docx, .pdf, .txt, or .rtf will allow more eyeballs and algorithms to see your content.

Length

Most recruiters recommend one page of content for every ten years of experience. In general, I share this perspective. Most recruiters will only look at the first page of your résumé. As an entry-level to mid-career person, this behavior doesn't matter as much. But for those with more experience to share, it can be tricky to pare down what you want a recruiter or hiring manager to see, or more so, what you want to MAKE SURE they see.

Major Sections

I break up the résumé into six major sections:

1. Personal Information
2. Headline
3. Core Competencies
4. (Relevant) Work Experience
5. Education
6. (Relevant) Personal Experience

Determining the order of these sections on a résumé depends on where you are in your career. In general, if you're a new grad, early in your career, making a career transition, or re-entering the workforce, your education should immediately follow your headline.

Note: I parenthesize "Relevant" as a reminder that anything and everything included on your résumé should be relevant to the job in question. Let's not forget *transferable skills*. There is an opportunity for you to call out transferable skills in most sections. We'll address this point specifically later on to give you an idea of what to be thinking about as you decide what to include and exclude for each applicable question.

What does each section consist of?

Personal Information

Simple stuff: Your full legal name, phone number, and email address are the bare minimum. I generally don't recommend including physical addresses anymore, especially in this era of remote work.

Headline

Your headline is a phrase of keywords that describes your value proposition. Examples include Senior Marketing Professional, Mid-Level Financial Analyst, and Early Career IT Specialist. I suggest indicating what "level" you are in your career, to suggest to your prospective employer that you're aware of where you fit in their organization and how what you can offer adds value. Also include the department or function your expertise falls into. This, again, demonstrates to your prospective employer your awareness of where you fit on their org chart and what you bring to the table.

LinkedIn has a field they too refer to as the Headline. In both instances, as a job seeker, I recommend this approach. It demystifies where you are on your career path and the industry/function in which you work.

In summary, your headline is an opportunity to succinctly distill your career chronicle to a plot summary that they can process in milliseconds.

Core Competencies

These are just what they sound like. Think both soft and hard skills. These include everything from software languages you can code in to systems you know how to use. They include general skills like marketing, branding, financial planning and analysis, benefits and compensation, training, leadership—the list goes on and on. The key is to be mindful of what you choose to exclude, as much as, if not more than, what you choose to include.

A tip: the earlier you are in your career, the more general and broad these terms will be.

Keep in mind that you only have so much space. Most recruiters and hiring managers don't (or rather, won't) look past the first page of your résumé. Make these count!

Transferable Skills

This is the most obvious place to showcase your transferable skills, as *competencies* is another word for skills. Include skills that transcend industries and functions. These might range from project management to pitching to operations management. To reiterate, focus on the role you're applying to and work backwards. How does your experience align with the skills required by this position? How does it fit in your professional narrative? What are the keywords you can include in this section that show the hiring manager and/or recruiter you have what it takes to perform the job well?

(Relevant) Work Experience

This section is the meat of your content. Notice the keyword *relevant* here. Remember, what you include is just as important as what you exclude.

Relevance will vary depending on the type of job you're applying for. For example, if you're applying for a sales position, you will include statistics related to any experience you have generating revenue, building a client base, upselling or cross-selling opportunities, etc. You won't include the fact that you led a project enhancing the workplace culture. Do you see the difference? While it's awesome that you led a project that likely affected the company in some valuable capacity, it isn't RELEVANT to the sales position you're applying for. Your résumé is valuable real estate. You don't need to add details that don't increase buyer interest or your overall value as a whole.

Transferable Skills

Another key section in which to showcase these. When you're first figuring out what is relevant, it can be challenging to figure this out *and* determine your transferable skills that are also relevant.

Remember to answer the following questions regarding your background and the job(s) in question:

1. Where is the overlap?
2. What similarities exist between these jobs? What are the differences?
3. How would you describe these similarities?

And, in addition:

4. How can you summarize the similarities in terms of skills and experiences?

In the "What to Include," section, we'll touch on how to quantify and qualify these skills and experiences in a way that resonates with hiring managers and recruiters.

Education

This section includes "education" in formal and informal contexts. Typically, we think of education in terms of institutions of higher learning, including junior colleges, four-year colleges, universities, graduate work, etc.

This section can also include any "boot camps," such as in software or programming, or "masterclasses" where the knowledge acquired is relevant to the job you're applying for. (Broken record, right?) If you have taken courses that aren't relevant to the job in question, I generally suggest erring on the side of excluding them. Remember, a résumé is your pitch sheet. When you get further along in the interview process, there will be a time to share other things, in this case, additional learning experiences.

The only exception to this are undergraduate and graduate degrees. Always include these. It shows your commitment to learning and arguably foundational skill sets. In Part III, we'll touch on how and why this may (or may not) change over time, but in today's landscape it's best to include them.

(Relevant) Personal Experience

I saved this for last because it's somewhat unorthodox and not something you see on résumés too often. This section includes anything that doesn't quite fit under any other section but that you feel is relevant to the job you're applying for.

A common example would be volunteer commitments. Speaking engagements are another. Maybe you're applying for a sales position, and you organized a neighborhood bake sale that generated a significant amount of revenue—this is where you can include that information. Again, because it's relevant and personal.

What to exclude

Remember, what you decide to exclude from your résumé could be more important than what you decide to include.

The Big Question

If you remember only one thing from this book, let it be this:

As you're curating your résumé content, for every piece of information you consider adding, ask yourself, *will the hiring manager or recruiter care?*

How do you know if they'll care or not? The job description. This is your best opportunity to understand and vet what the employer would like to see in their ideal candidate. Again, this is where relevance is key. As a job seeker, it's your responsibility to ensure the hiring manager and/or recruiter has the information they need to make a **favorable** decision about your candidacy.

> As you're curating your résumé content, for every piece of information you consider adding, ask yourself, *will the hiring manager or recruiter care?*

The Big Answer

How do you do that? Try this exercise.

1. Start with the current version of your résumé. (If you don't have one, take this opportunity to write down a few bullet points based on the major sections you're considering including. (Relevant) work experience is a good place to start.

2. For each bullet, ask yourself:
    a. Will the hiring manager or recruiter care about this information?
        i. If yes, congrats! Move on to the next.
        ii. If no, ask yourself, *how can I update this information to make it relevant?* If you can't make it relevant, take it out.
3. When in doubt, leave it out!

I know this sounds counterintuitive, but you'll find it's much easier to include relevant details when you take this approach.

What to include

"Relevant"

What does "relevant" really mean? It means that in some obvious way, the information relates to the job you're applying for AND shows the hiring manager and/or recruiter you are qualified for the job.

In English class, we learn to "show, not tell" when we're writing stories. The same idea applies to writing your résumé. *Show* the employer you're qualified for the job using relevant examples. Alluding to the sections we touched on, your headline, core competencies, work experience, education, and personal experience should

You should hire me for this job and here's why!

illustrate your qualifications and convey a consistent narrative with the plotline of, *You should hire me for this job and here's why!*

A tip: read through the job description and circle the keywords. What are keywords? Words or phrases that appear multiple times in the document. Figure out how to integrate these into your résumé so they support your narrative. This goes without saying: never lie on your résumé.

Quantitative versus qualitative

While your résumé is a narrative, it's also a pitch sheet. What does that mean? It means you need to distill your qualifications succinctly and package them so the hiring manager and/or recruiter can pretty much immediately make a favorable judgement on your candidacy.

Use numbers whenever and wherever possible. Numbers capture our achievements better than words, and I'm saying that as a writer! Some achievements are easier to quantify than others, such as sales, accounting, and marketing. Depending on your experience and your intended next role, you might need to think outside the box.

What numbers are we talking about?

- Dollars (revenue generated, costs saved, budgets managed, ROI)
- Percentages (growth, shrinkage)

- Ranking (your place on a team, and/or based on performance)
- Time (you saved the company, length of a project)

Also consider rates like retention, turnover, the sizes of teams you've managed, the number of hires you've made, and the contributions of teams you've overseen.

So many jobs are cross-functional now that most of your impact will likely be as part of a greater role. Understand your role in terms of the team, department, and organization, and identify where your contributions are so you can distill them in a way that conveys your value and your skill set. Think about the company's challenges and how you helped address or solve them. What innovations (tech, systems, protocols, products, programs) did you introduce? What policies and/or procedures did you create, implement or enhance?

SNAPSHOT: COVER LETTER

Cover letters are the epitome of professional narrative in the traditional sense. They have a beginning, a middle, and end, all of which, if done correctly, fit together to tell the story of why you're the best candidate for the opportunity in question.

In general, the simplest framework for a cover letter is this:

Beginning: Why you're writing, what job you're applying for, how you're qualified for the job

Middle: Examples that illustrate why you're the best candidate and how your qualifications address the company's needs/solve their problems

End: Reiteration of why you're writing, what job you're applying for, and how you're qualified for the job

Generally, I recommend keeping cover letters between 300 and 500 words. Remember, hiring teams read a lot of these, therefore brevity and clarity are appreciated. Why say what you need to in 1,000 words when you can use 400?

The examples you use *should* be referenced somewhere on your résumé. This creates a cohesiveness that allows hiring teams to make connections easier. Repetition of key facts increases the likelihood that a recruiter will remember this information, which is in your best interest as a candidate. Remember to use numbers in your examples and show why and how your contributions are meaningful and what impact you made. How are they measurable? Show this in your story.

SNAPSHOT: LINKEDIN PROFILE

LinkedIn has evolved a lot since its launch in 2002. I made my own profile in 2009, while I was still in college. The purpose of your profile from a career-chronicle standpoint is, again, to share your professional narrative in a way that showcases your value and how you've made positive impacts in previous workplaces, communities, educational forums, etc.

There are several sections on the LinkedIn Profile interface we won't go into detail on, as these sections often change names and are added or subtracted.

Generally speaking, a few tips to keep in mind when writing your content focus on, you guessed it, the narrative.

For example, use the About/Summary section to share a short bio about your career path. Use keywords for opportunities you're looking for or aspire to so that you're more searchable for those trying to find people like you. Again, keep it short and to the point, about 500 words or less if you can.

Pay attention to the Skills & Endorsements section. Make sure they reflect your competencies and interests. The top three spots should correspond to your top three skills.

Look at job descriptions of roles you're applying for or that are comparable to your current role or your next forecasted role. (You should always pay attention to the job market, titles of jobs, etc., as things change so quickly these days. This is the best way to be proactive in your career.) Get an understanding of how these job descriptions represent their roles and responsibilities, and use that to inform how you structure your narrative. Don't copy them, but use them as a resource to help you share your narrative and convey how you add value.

TAKEAWAYS

Remember, you're building your professional narrative, your career chronicle. Tell a story with your content. Include only the details that will matter to the hiring manager or recruiter. Use numbers whenever and wherever possible. Consult the job description for inspiration and leads on what to include and exclude.

PART III: PLANNING FOR THE (NEAR AND DISTANT) FUTURE

Careers are fickle things. Whether we like it or not, what we now consider "a stable career" isn't what it used to be, or what our parents or grandparents might have considered a stable career.

Change is ever-present and not going away. While this idea can be overwhelming and overstimulating at times, it's in our best interest to be aware of it, accept it, and make adaptations as best as we can.

Here is an excerpt from my book, *The Mind Is Just Like A Muscle*. This section describes "the internet effect:"

THE INTERNET EFFECT

The term "internet effect" as used here is a reference to the consequences of the latest revolutionary technologies—namely, the internet—on how humans think.

How we consume information has evolved as a result of inventions, advancements, and changes such as the printing press, the television, and most recently, the internet. Human history can be time stamped in three revolutions:

1. The Cognitive Revolution
2. The Agricultural Revolution
3. The Scientific Revolution

We could say that we are still living in the Scientific Revolution. During this era, we have witnessed the birth of the internet and its immediate consequences. To make it simple, let's say the internet started making a notable impact beginning in 2000. If we assume that anyone born in the Generation Z demographic (born between 1997-2012) and later "grew up with the internet," we're talking about 23% of the American population. If we assume anyone born in the Generation Y demographic (born between 1981-1996) and later "grew up with the internet," we're talking about 47% of the American population. For Gen Y, the internet became a daily feature around high school or college; for Gen Z, it was elementary or middle school—very different yet formative periods in a lifetime. Of today's living population in America, about half grew up with the internet. Today, 50% of 11-year-olds have their own cell phone.

Social media is a by-product of the internet, as are many products and services available to us in the forms of devices (I see you, Apple) and ecommerce platforms (Amazon). Once might even call these inventions "distractions". As Nicholas Carr describes it in his book on this topic, The Shallows: What the Internet Is Doing to Our Brains,

"The distractions in our lives have been proliferating for a long time, but never has there been a medium that, like the Net, has been programmed to so widely scatter our attention and to do it so insistently."

A vulnerability of human psychology is centered around this impulse, our innate human need for gratification. Social media platforms, like the long-gone Myspace and the more long-standing (i.e., still surviving) Facebook, Instagram, Twitter, and YouTube (and more recently still, TikTok), are great examples of this, but there are other more "useful" technologies that also exploit this human weakness.

Consider the GPS. While helpful for navigation, there are times when these systems break down: they don't have sufficient mapping capabilities; the address is incorrect and you wind up somewhere else unintentionally; it says to make a U-turn when you know you can just go left and arrive at your destination.

The point is, we have these great, complex brains, and yet sometimes we let things take advantage of them and override their capabilities and strengths. The challenge is having the awareness to realize when this is happening, and adjust accordingly. In a word, exercise.

It's also possible that the depth of our intelligence is shifting. Humans used to define intelligence as the extent to which a person had a mind capable of sitting quietly and solving complex problems. However, after the Industrial Revolution, a new definition of intelligence started to take hold—one that privileged efficiency and multi-tasking over deep thinking. We can think about these types of intelligence 1) as shallow and wide, and 2) narrow and deep. With the invention of the internet, our obsession with efficiency has spiraled out of control. Our applications, platforms, and digital tools are so quick and easy to use that we have become obsessed with being better, faster, stronger—but at what cost? The volume of data we are exposed to when we surf the web may be impressive, but our brains are not equipped to both navigate the distractions inherent in the design of the internet and consolidate deep and meaningful new elements of knowledge. Increased reliance on the internet has induced what can be called "an age of distraction," resulting in our own inability to find a balance between being thoughtful and solutions-oriented and fast and efficient, in a world now dictated by the computer and its accessories.

Consider that there are now entire careers devoted to this. User experience, or UX, design is just one. 85% of jobs that will exist in 2030 haven't even been invented yet. That's a direct result of the speed at which technology changes how we approach and perform work. (I've written quite a few blog posts on this topic. Please see the Appendix for a few selections about the future of work.)

As with psychological projection, the internet effect isn't a bias, but it exposes limitations of the human brain that can result in less-than-optimum consequences if we're not mindful of how to manage its impact.

THE BRAIN IS JUST LIKE A MUSCLE

Based on the research, bias may be natural to us, but our consciousness gives us the benefit of awareness if we're willing to exercise our brains. After all, the brain is more than a keeper of intelligence. The brain is just like a muscle. Building awareness is like building muscle—only in our cranium, and not on our biceps. It's a strength that will help us in the long run. If we don't maintain it, it will atrophy and go limp.

As change takes on the most amplified and version of itself, so too are we tasked with responding to what differences change itself leaves in its wake.

These include, as far as the workplace is concerned:

1. New technologies, which build . . .
2. New systems, which lead to . . .
3. New processes, which affect . . .
4. How companies do business with their employees and customers.

Sara Salam

WHAT DOES IT MEAN TO BE "QUALIFIED" FOR A JOB?

While there are a lot of jobs open—6.6 million, as reported by the Bureau of Labor Statistics on the last business day of December 2020—we are seeing an increasingly **wide gap** between the jobs being created, and the skills and experiences in the workforce needed to fill them.

Simply put, there are more jobs than there are "qualified people" to fill them. What makes someone qualified for a job?

Whether we like it or not, we are living in an era where **reskilling** and **upskilling** ourselves is crucial to our employability and marketability as members of the workforce. We constantly need to learn the latest technologies and newest apps in order to meet the needs of our employers.

Unfortunately, what's happening right now is employers don't have a firm grasp of how to navigate this evolution of the talent marketplace. How could they? It's never happened before in the history of humankind—at least in the way it's happening now.

Even so, for employers, today's hiring approach begs rethinking how talent is viewed. But how?

For starters, being "qualified" for a job no longer *directly correlates* to years of experience or the type of degree one holds. These things may be relevant, but are not a determinant of success in a job, according to statistics.

How to Write a Résumé

Today, being "qualified" correlates to:

1. Willingness to learn
2. Adaptability to the needs of the business
3. Ability to think critically and problem solve

Most of the high-demand positions today are in software, service, sales, engineering, design, and other digitally-enabled roles. Data shows that healthcare jobs and eldercare are also in great demand.

The big question for employers is, how do we catch up to the demand of the job market when the current supply of talent isn't cutting it?

The short answer for employers is to re-evaluate what makes someone "qualified" for their open jobs, given this new reality of work, and adjust their hiring process accordingly.

Mercer anticipates 65% of current primary school children will have jobs that don't even exist yet.

That's insane! How can we continue with our current antics knowing past experience will be all but irrelevant for our future workforce not fifteen years down the road?

In an interview with Harvard Business Review, executive search adviser Claudio Fernández-Aráoz explains the inherent challenges the people making hiring decisions face today (i.e., having the wrong brain, the wrong software, and the wrong focus) and why hiring for potential over past performance is critical to the future of business.

The key to matching talent with the right job hinges on determining what components of the job can and cannot be taught. It's nature versus nurture on a whole new level.

The rub is this: while we are all human, we are each unique in our brain biology and our behaviors, and how these factors translate into the workplace. As our brains develop through our teen years, our neurons make connections to create mental pathways that eventually shape the way we think and view the world. This is how we create our sense, our unique network of connections specific to our individual experience of how we understand and interact with the world.

Therefore, we each have something different to offer, to share, to teach—and the issue in the workplace is that many employers don't know how to figure out what that is WITHOUT using past experience as a reference. (That's what a résumé is, after all. Don't they exist for a reason?)

I'm not suggesting that employers should make a 180-degree change in their hiring practices *tomorrow*. I'm suggesting employers should consider the long-term goals (looking ahead five to ten years, or more) for their organization, and given the changing landscape of the business world, reassess how human capital will contribute to and impact the goals of the company. From there, they can design plans for a shift (or shifts) in people resources and repurpose or realign positions.

This is probably one of the most difficult things a company has to do: determine how to allocate its resources, people or otherwise. It also defines whether a company succeeds or fails. The challenge of staffing, talent acquisition, recruiting—whatever you want to call it—is becoming infinitely more complex, and it's not going to get any less so, but the mission is to figure out ways to manage the complexity and tame its potentially detrimental implications if not addressed effectively.

Fernández-Aráoz says we need to focus on figuring out how to select people who are open to learning, and also on knowing what they will need to learn as they move forward in their careers.

But for now, I challenge you to consider what about your job can and can't be taught. Does your job allow you to learn in a way that jives with your natural behavior? If yes, you're likely in the right job. If no, you might have some soul-searching to do.

ROLE OF EDUCATION

Not too long ago, and arguably still the case for some employers, having at least a four-year degree from an institution of higher learning could have been considered a baseline requirement for many salaried positions. When I was in high school, the importance of a college degree could not be understated. I'm not making a judgement on the value of higher education. People with advanced degrees play a big role in our society and that will continue to be true. Access to information, however, has drastically accelerated, and with that, so has the opportunity to educate ourselves in less-formal settings and by less formal or structured means.

Over the last several years, with the proliferation of platforms that host "edutainment" content, continuous learning has increased in scale and access. While many people in the world still don't have access to the internet, there are many that do. If you're looking to upskill or reskill yourself in a particular field or subject or vocation, there are many sources—both paid and unpaid—that you can access to supplement your knowledge base and skill set.

As with anything, be mindful of the platforms you use or pay for and the sources from which you get your information. Make sure they're credible. Do your research. Ask questions.

Many employers tend to favor certifications from credentialed organizations. We can speculate for hours about why one employer might accept one type of certification while another might not. Remember to focus on your overall professional narrative and what your goals are. Remind yourself of your "why." Consistently check in with yourself to make sure you're on track. We tend to deviate sometimes, and that's okay; the key is to be aware of how you're progressing (or not) and what the consequences are. Only you can decide what's right for you.

ROLE OF THE RÉSUMÉ

Leonardo da Vinci is credited with having crafted the first modern résumé. Consider the below excerpt from a letter he addressed to the Duke of Milan, where Leonardo captured his achievements in developing war instruments—presumably in an attempt to secure a job:

"Where the operation of bombardment might fail, I would contrive catapults, mangonels, trabocchi, and other machines of marvellous efficacy and not in common use. And in short, according to the variety of cases, I can contrive various and endless means of offense and defense."

We could venture to say that the job market in Leonardo's day was relatively stable, in that the variance of skills and experience within a given labor market was limited.

Today, however, job responsibilities themselves skew broadly, because the rapid pace of change (cue technology) has shifted what work those jobs are needed to perform.

Today, some examples of those jobs might include a drone pilot—or drone fleet manager, for that matter—or an autonomous transportation specialist. No member of the workforce has this specific work background, because this work has never existed until now.

Now consider the following:

As I mentioned in the excerpt from my book, *The Mind Is Just Like A Muscle*, the Institute for the Future (IFTF) estimates 85% of jobs that will exist in 2030 haven't even been invented yet—a reality that significantly departs from the world Leonardo was living in.

In today's world, the past experience documented by résumés doesn't necessarily correlate with future performance in an obvious way. As we've noted, the scope of work is decidedly uncertain and subject to constant change.

What is certain is that humans have great capacity to learn new things, and should be matched with jobs based on this capacity.

> "Potential is not fixed. We believe in human beings' ability to grow; society cannot achieve economic as well as cultural progress without it . . . They can and do reinvent themselves."
> –The Leadership Pipeline

"Should" is a subjective claim. Given this evolving landscape, the key for job seekers is to illustrate their transferable and relevant skills, to show their prospective employer how their background aligns with their prospective employer's needs. It starts with the professional narrative—the career chronicle.

"Potential is not fixed. We believe in human beings' ability to grow; society cannot achieve economic as well as cultural progress without it... They can and do reinvent themselves."—The Leadership Pipeline.

THE FUTURE OF JOB HUNTING

As we mentioned in the introduction, while we can't predict what will happen, the future of job hunting will likely be dictated by a combination of market forces, technology, and the pace of adaptation of technology by employers and job seekers alike.

Adaptation, I'd argue, is probably the most inconsistent when it comes to how it affects job seekers in this context. This is one of the aspects we cannot control on an individual level. How Company A might implement one piece of software used to screen applicants could be different from how Company B might use the same software. This is one reason the résumé has stayed relevant for as long as it has; everybody has one, and generally knows what it should include (though there are better, more effective ways to build one than others, as you've learned).

Some ATSs use search engine optimization, while others don't. Some ATSs only show the first page of a résumé, where others have a flipping feature.

Referrals, or knowing someone connected to an employer, will always be part of the hiring process. You can't control that. What you can control is how you market yourself as the best candidate for the job in question.

THE ULTIMATE QUESTION: HOW DO WE STAY RELEVANT?

Relevance, as we've homed in on through much of this text, is the key to communicating our value in the workplace. It's as much about communicating our value to our potential employer(s) as it's about understanding our value ourselves.

My hypothesis is that our ability to reskill and upskill will dictate our career trajectories in the future. In fact, it's happening now, participating in companies that value training, learning, and development. While previously these departments/offerings/programs might have been considered "nice to have," I'd argue that as we move forward, they will be essential for retention and keeping up with business demand... and relevance. It all comes full circle.

How can you stay skilled and relevant as jobs evolve and change? One of the great advantages of the modern era is our access to information:

1. Take a class (or several). Non-paid (YouTube—I taught myself how to sketch!) or paid (MasterClass, Coursera, Teachable) classes are great opportunities to refine, develop, or learn a new skill. Consider looking into a local community college's course offerings, too.
2. Read. There is so much knowledge out there that's documented in books, magazines, periodicals, journals, and the like. I'd suggest focusing on accredited sources versus whatever pops up first in

your Google search. While we have amazing access to information, it's just as important to be mindful of where that information comes from.

3. Informational Meetings. Notice I didn't say *interviews* or *networking events*. These are a great way to learn about the inner workings of a company and ask how it's changed over a period of time. Ideally, you'd want to chat with someone who has been around for some meaty changes in a company's history, such as a merger and acquisition, leadership transition, etc. These conversations will help you understand what it looks like on the ground, and might help you down the road should an opportunity arise that suits your background and interests!
4. Learn a new language. In our increasingly interconnected world, the ability to speak multiple languages will eventually become a necessity. (In some industries, it already is.) This ability not only makes you a more desirable candidate for job opportunities, it expands your opportunities for work with an international scope, including government, international trade, politics, cinema, food production, etc.

WHAT WE CAN CONTROL

We can control how we respond. That's it, and that's all.

There will always be changes in how businesses hire, how job seekers search, where people live, and how much they earn. If recent history, or the past thirty years, is any indication, change is accelerating, and managing our expectations is a challenge, to say the least.

While we aren't able to control the pace that Change affects us, we can control how we respond. We can reskill ourselves. We can educate ourselves about the gaps that need filling, and find ways to fill those gaps. That, in a nutshell, is the future.

> While we aren't able to control the pace that Change affects us, we can control how we respond. We can reskill ourselves. We can educate ourselves about the gaps that need filling, and find ways to fill those gaps. That, in a nutshell, is the future.

I suggest pairing the strategies in this book with other job searching strategies, including but not limited to:

- How to master the informational interview
- How to leverage existing relationships (strong and weak ties) to get a job interview
- How to interview effectively
- How to negotiate a job offer

- How to get the information you need to make a decision on a job offer

It's critical we take ownership of our careers by understanding what we can control. The more effective you are in communicating your value, the more likely an employer will understand your value, too.

CONCLUSION

My intent in writing and curating this book is to help job seekers who are looking for inspiration on how to refresh their approach to the job search process. While this book focuses on career chronicle content, it also shows job seekers a different way of approaching the job hunting process and how to present themselves to employers.

We've seen there's really no good or bad time to be in the job market in absolute terms. It depends on the industry and microtrends that relate to your core skills and experience.

We've learned the significance of transferable skills, and that understanding how to convey your value in terms of numbers and relevant experience helps communicate your professional narrative.

We've learned what you exclude from your narrative may be more important than what you include.

We've speculated about the future of work and what we can do to prepare for it.

We've reminded ourselves it's important to focus on what we can control.

Your career chronicle is but one part of the job search process. Don't forget to research and educate yourself on the other critical parts, as mentioned in Part III. If you're stuck or need additional resources, feel free to contact me at bysarasalam.com/careerconsulting and we'll figure it out together.

Now, go get 'em!

BONUS CONTENT

BLOG: GHOSTED: THE JOB SEEKER'S DILEMMA

Originally published September 21, 2019

Ghosting job applicants has become a prevalent phenomenon in the hiring process. In fact, 75% of job seekers say they never hear back from a job they applied for.

During a time when unemployment is low, which should be a good thing , candidates are suffering from a nascent behavior that was once solely associated with online dating.

This ghosting behavior is now characteristic of employers worldwide, who manage applicant pools of sometimes thousands of people.

These people are represented by a line on an Excel spreadsheet, a hyperlink on a dashboard, or a digitized résumé. The point is, employers are so overwhelmed by the sheer volume of hungry job seekers, they disregard the human behind the hyperlink.

Most times, this is completely unintentional. We live in a world where we have 11 million bits of stimuli (it's true!) coming our way at any given moment. How could recruiters and hiring managers possibly view all the résumés AND make time to get back to everyone on their status?

Our grandparents saw as many people in one month as we do in one day. Our innate biology struggles to keep up with this avalanche of data—a recent development as of the past twenty years, which is a conservative estimate of time.

This is a big reason why at least 30% of hires today are based on referrals. Referrals allow us to bypass a few steps of analysis, which is taxing for our brains, and speed up what could otherwise be a very lengthy hiring process. (Most already are.)

How do we address this problem?

For employers, reduce your barriers and sync up whatever systems you're using to track your candidates. Ask your IT department to install a widget. Designate an HR Coordinator to send communications on the start date of each new hire to officially close the open req. In this technological age, there is a solution to this problem. You need to take responsibility for it.

For job seekers, accept the current state of things and keep up your search, no matter how discouraging it may be.

BLOG: MAKE IT WORK

Originally published September 25, 2019

Today, work transcends our professional and personal lives. Many of us take work calls on vacation, send emails in transit between the office and home (dangerous, and not recommended), or most simply, some days we work from home. It can't get much more integrated than that—blending your personal space with your work space.

Frequently, we forget that those running our businesses are human beings. First and foremost, before we are employees, before we are business owners, we are human beings. We all have physical needs, mental needs, emotional needs, etc., that don't disappear once work begins.

As humans navigating this landscape, it's critical we recognize what fundamentally makes us human, what are the unique characteristics that define the human condition, and what the implications are for us at work, and quite frankly, at home as well.

Today I'm sharing three sources, literary edition, that get at this idea and explain how simply being aware of our humanity can help us be happier and more effective at work, and by extension, life in general.

Point No. 1: Human nature is not one-size-fits-all.

"The power of human nature is that, unlike any other forces of nature, it is not uniform. Instead, its power lies in its idiosyncrasy—in the fact that each human's nature is different. If companies want to use this power, they must find a mechanism to unleash each human's nature, not contain it."—First, Break All The Rules

Everyone has a different nature, different strengths, different things that make us great. Nike rolled out a campaign in 2012 called "Find Your Greatness." It highlights exactly this concept—that everyone is different, and everyone can be great. It's about identifying what that greatness is, and creating your value around it. If people are in roles that bring out their best selves, productivity becomes a given and not an obstacle. That means treating people fairly, but not the same, as one size does not fit all.

Point No. 2: Our potential and capacity to learn is not static, but dynamic.

"Potential is not fixed. We believe in human beings' ability to grow; society cannot achieve economic as well as cultural progress without it….They can and do reinvent themselves."—The Leadership Pipeline

While each of our natural behaviors are ingrained and our brains primed at an early age, we as humans are capable of acquiring knowledge and developing skills. Both knowledge and skills contribute to the advancement and growth of ourselves, and as each individual experiences this progress, we all grow and develop together as a civilization and culture. We become better marketers, better accountants, better leaders, better parents, better friends. Life is a learning opportunity, and in understanding this we should design in our companies and positions inherent ways to expand on what we know and apply what we learn. This could take the form of focus groups, innovation tournaments, and the like. The key is to keep these opportunities consistent to show them as recognized human needs that are important to address.

Point No. 3: Self-examination is uniquely human.

"We need to stop asking about the meaning of life, and instead think of ourselves as those who were being questioned by life . . ." —Man's Search For Meaning

Sometimes we get in our own heads and rethink everything. Surprise—this is a uniquely human trait, unshared by any other mammal or living species (that we're aware of). While this feature allows us to examine our options and make decisions based on those options, it can sometimes paralyze our progress when we "think too much." Recalling an earlier post on indecision, we need to be mindful of our actions (or lack thereof), own our choices, and be accountable for our purpose. When we define our purpose in relation to our jobs, we satisfy our human desire for meaning, for fulfillment, for being a part of something bigger than ourselves.

Tying these three points together, whether or home or in the office, humans need opportunities to figure out who they are and what they need to be successful without risk of recourse or punishment. Sometimes our society's expectations and standards for behavior run counter to exactly this idea. We need to make conscious choices to either align ourselves with these, or run the opposite way in pursuit of something different—something more human.

So, everyone, I challenge you to explore more about yourself and what makes you great, and how that value translates both personally for you and your self-awareness as a human being, and professionally as you maximize your performance in the workplace. And employers, I challenge you to show your people you understand their human needs, and create ways for them to discover how they can best be an asset to you in ways that also make them happy and fulfilled.

Because all human beings should feel safe and empowered in pursuit of their dreams.

THANK YOU!

I am so appreciative of you taking the time to read this book. I hope you found value in its content.

If you enjoyed *How to Write a Résumé*, and would be willing to spare just two or three minutes... please share your review of the book on my website:

www.bysarasalam.com

Reviews help me get the book into as many hands as possible, and support my work as an author for the long-term (my dream!).

I'm grateful for your support and look forward to sharing more of my work with you!

ACKNOWLEDGMENTS

After working in human resources and recruitment for the better part of ten years, I felt compelled to share the knowledge and observations I've acquired about a topic that most adults experience: the job search. As an author, writing a book to capture this information seemed like the way to go.

I wrote this book for all the job seekers who don't know where to start, who know where to start but don't know what to do next, who need a new perspective on job hunting, who need a little bit of hope in an oftentimes disheartening process.

As with all my work, especially nonfiction and self-help, I'm grateful for the opportunity to share my perspectives in a manner that's thoughtful and inquisitive, while also admitting there's so much we're still learning and so much that will continue to evolve and change, as jobs are created, as jobs disappear, as our world reinvents itself in perpetuity.

And as always, I'm grateful for the support of family and friends who motivate me to keep going.

ABOUT THE AUTHOR

Sara Salam is an award-winning author, poet, and editor. Published since age 11, Sara writes nonfiction, fiction, and poetry. In *How to Write a Résumé*, Sara uses her experiences as a ten-year Human Resources professional, recruiter and consultant to help job seekers think about and approach the job hunting process in a different way. Sara enjoys writing, yoga and the beach. Connect with Sara at:

www.bysarasalam.com/careerconsulting

© 2021 Sara Salam

🌐 www.bysarasalam.com/careerconsulting

📷 @bysarasalam

▶ Sara Salam

REFERENCES

Adecco Staffing, U. (2016, June 07). Cost of employee turnover calculator: Adecco. Retrieved January 03, 2021, from https://www.adeccousa.com/employers/resources/cost-of-turnover-calculator/

Barstow, S. (2019, February 12). Ideal overhead percentage. Retrieved January 02, 2021, from https://smallbusiness.chron.com/ideal-overhead-percentage-75876.html

Bellis, R. (2017, September 07). The war for talent is over, and everyone lost. Retrieved January 03, 2021, from https://www.fastcompany.com/3069078/the-war-for-talent-is-over-and-everyone-lost

Dishman, L. (2015, September 01). Why companies make bad hires. Retrieved January 16, 2021, from https://www.fastcompany.com/3050570/why-companies-make-bad-hires

Dodson, C. (2015, June 18). Why you should treat your employees like your most loyal customers. Retrieved January 03, 2021, from https://www.fastcompany.com/3047366/why-you-should-treat-your-employees-like-your-most-loyal-customers

Fatemi, F. (2016, September 29). The true cost of a bad hire -- it's more than you think. Retrieved January 02, 2021, from https://www.forbes.com/sites/falonfatemi/2016/09/28/the-true-cost-of-a-bad-hire-its-more-than-you-think/?sh=51c59b814aa4

Fernández-Aráoz, C. (2014, June 03). Hire for potential, not just experience. Retrieved January 03, 2021, from https://hbr.org/video/3603876266001/hire-for-potential-not-just-experience

Glassdoor: 50 HR and Recruiting Stats That Make You Think. (2018). Retrieved January 03, 2021, from https://b2b-assets.glassdoor.com/50-hr-and-recruiting-stats.pdf

Investopedia: Guide to Unemployment. (2020, July 28). Retrieved January 02, 2021, from https://www.investopedia.com/

Job seeker nation Study 2016. (2019, May 18). Retrieved January 02, 2021, from https://www.jobvite.com/job-seeker-nation-study-2016/

Kolko, J. (2020, December 01). 2020 US labor Market review and 2021 Outlook. Retrieved January 02, 2021, from https://www.hiringlab.org/2020/12/01/2020-labor-market-review-2021-outlook/

Ladders: Eye-Tracking Study. (2018). Retrieved January 03, 2021, from https://www.theladders.com/static/images/basicSite/pdfs/TheLadders-EyeTracking-StudyC2.pdf

Linkedin: Global Recruiting Trends 2017. (2017). Retrieved January 03, 2021, from https://business.linkedin.com/content/dam/me/business/en-us/talent-solutions/resources/pdfs/linkedin-global-recruiting-trends-report.pdf

A short history of corporations. (2002, July 05). Retrieved January 03, 2021, from https://newint.org/features/2002/07/05/history

Sinek, S. (2009, September). How great leaders inspire action. Retrieved January 03, 2021, from https://www.ted.com/talks/simon_sinek_how_great_leaders_inspire_action?language=en

State of the American Workplace (Rep.). (2017). Gallup.

Tarki, A., Sanandaji, T., & Francis, B. (2020, October 22). Why hiring During Covid is different than in previous downturns. Retrieved January 02, 2021, from https://hbr.org/2020/10/why-hiring-during-covid-is-different-than-in-previous-downturns

Total unfilled job vacancies for the United States. (2021, January 21). Retrieved January 04, 2021, from https://fred.stlouisfed.org/series/LMJVTTUVUSM647S

U.S. Bureau of Labor Statistics. (2021, February 24). Retrieved January 02, 2021, from https://www.bls.gov/

Why new hires fail. (n.d.). Retrieved January 04, 2021, from https://www.leadershipiq.com/blogs/leadershipiq/35354241-why-new-hires-fail-emotional-intelligence-vs-skills

World Economic Forum: Chapter 1: The future of jobs and skills. (2016). Retrieved January 03, 2021, from https://reports.weforum.org/future-of-jobs-2016/chapter-1-the-future-of-jobs-and-skills/

The world's first resume Is 500-years old and still can teach you a lesson or two. (2015). Retrieved January 03, 2021, from https://business.linkedin.com/talent-solutions/blog/recruiting-humor-and-fun/2015/the-worlds-first-resume-is-500-years-old

www.ingramcontent.com/pod-product-compliance
Lightning Source LLC
Chambersburg PA
CBHW021449070526
44577CB00002B/330